Poems Last Longer Than Roses

Rachel Green

Presentation by *BookLeaf Publishing*

Web: www.bookleafpub.com

E-mail: info@bookleafpub.com

ISBN: 978-93-95755-69-6

First edition 2022

*To my heart, for surviving what my brain
never thought i could.*

ACKNOWLEDGEMENT

To everyone, including myself that I Love, thank you for your inspiration.

Emerging

She just appears ...
Slowly waking up in the tall grass,
surrounded by flowers,
The scents of her surroundings slowly invade the
air she breathes ...
She smiles ...
She takes in the trees around her,
The flowers as they whisper words if wisdom,
It feels like home...she belongs here,
The light from the sun makes sprites dance
along her skin giving her an eternal glow
Her wings glitter and shine as she rises.

Love Kisses

The sweetest lie she has ever told,
Were those red lipstick stains,
Marks that trailed straight to her heart,
Sweet smiles and evil behind her eyes
She leaves a mess of broken and bloody remains
Of past lovers and empty promises
Of the sweetest lies she's ever told.

4:48am The Birds

These birds, these damn birds,
Yet despite their annoying chirp so early,
That's keeping me wide eyed and awake,
This feeling I get to silence them,
All I really need to do is roll over and snuggle
besides you,
Because all the noise fades,
within the sound of your heartbeat, resonating
deep within my head,
Lulling me to blissful sleep.

SunNight

The one night I couldn't sleep,
And I didn't wanna wake you,
So I waited until morning light,
To lay in bed besides you,
Falling asleep to the light snores
Of your peaceful slumber.

Thinking of me

I know you're thinking of me
With those intimate moments,
During your solo indulgence,
The sounds resonating,
Feelings still there,
Tracing across your mind
The way my hands ran across your body
As the sweat dripped off your flesh,
The euphoric feeling of ecstasy,
Rolling through you over and over,
Don't stop, can't stop, won't stop,
You keep going on and on,
Vibrations through your lips,
You pretend it's still me,
you see me, feel me, want me,
The epitome of your every desire you lust,
movements mimicked, faster now,
Switch the pace, harder now,
The sounds of your wetness,
It makes you hot, breath quickens,
Legs start to shake, you say my name,
Ocean waves crash through your body,
That arch you make so sexy,
Winding down, slower now,
You climax again,

with my face in your mind,
Satisfaction spreads across your face,
I know your sill thinking of me.

Ablaze

Behind her eyes,
There's a fire in her
That you never knew existed
Until her gaze lit up
Into your once empty soul.

Sunsets

I want sunsets on the beach
The scent of salt and palm trees in the wind
Long walks with sand squishing between my
toes
The gentle sea breeze blowing against my skin
Creating goosebumps across smooth flesh
The sky in an array of pinks yellows and oranges
Sun kissing the horizon before she falls asleep
Like a sensual show of love before the darkness
shines with her beautiful madness
I want sunsets on the beach with the scent of salt
palm trees and you ...

Stay

3am wrapped in your arms,
Our Legs intertwined,
Exchanging body heat,
my face buried into your neck,
Your breathing slowly syncing with mines,
Hands caressing in slow motions,
Sharing secrets we only confided to the stars,
As the moon and the stars sparkle in the sky,
Giving your skin an unearthly glow,
That moment of peace as we start to fall asleep,
Within the safety of your arms,
That's where I wanna stay.

The Birds - 4:48 pt2.

The birds,
No matter where I am
No matter how i feel
Same spot on the clock
Exact time on the dot
They never fail to speak up.

Away

As I stare into a sky filled with clouded past memories, I can't help to think that only a few hundred miles away I looked up into the same sky and felt something completely different then how I feel now under the never changing stars.

Vibes

In a second you turned my world upside down,
Revolutionized my inner being,
Captivated my soul and made her dance,
Making what was once thought of as unseemly
appalling so breathtakingly awe-inspiring,
Made dreams into reality,
My words now have true meaning,
Now understanding the words I've written in the
past,
The dreams I've wished i had,
Seemed like they weren't meant for anybody
until I had the privilege to meet you .
Vibes never recognized,
calling towards each other like an invisible pull,
red strings tied together so tight,
The universe doesn't wish it to unravel

Sleepless

5am,
Couldn't sleep,
Hazy smoke,
Birds saying Good Morning,
Coffee,
And thoughts of you.

Chasing Sleep

Every morning when she leaves the bed,
I snuggle up on her pillow
Just so I could be closer to her dreams .

Dont wake up yet.

15

You are every nightmare that I ever dreamed of,
And I say it in the most positive and in love
sense possible
For my nightmares are the perfection of
happiness, of every good feeling imaginable,
And I'm afraid to lose it all in the process of
waking up.
That's the real nightmare.

When We Grow Old

I wonder ..
When we are old , slightly crazy and in our
rocking chairs,
Would you make me blush,
The same way you do now?

Her and I

I inhale her scent ... She smells of cuban, dove,
and me. Like late nights, weed smoke,
unforgettable moments and me. Where she lived
and loved and didn't give a care in the world
with me. She slept and dreamt of fairy tales
turned into reality where I'm the damsel In
distress, Prince Charming wears a bra and it
proves permanent ink wrong. Leaves me
speechless ... How it's her and just ... Well me

Fear

I'm afraid to tell you that I Possibly love you,
Because for some reason like a fucked up curse,
Everything I love eventually
Leaves ....

138

You asked me the other day if I kept count ...
I turned away and shyly said no,
Truth is I have written you over 138 poems up to
date ...
One poem for each day ...
And counting ...

When We Grow Older

I wonder if we'd ever meet again in the future
and grow old together like you wanted ..
I wonder if it ever crosses your thoughts.

Do you still want that now?

Demons

Her demons control everything she does
And frankly ... Im in love with them

Confessions

By the time you're reading this I would have
died from embarrassment but eff it I'm trying to
be romantic
With or without you i am complete,
But With you i am completely happy,
For someone who writes im at a loss for words
that'll make sense,
This is harder then I thought, but okay, here it
goes:
I have wished that i met you sooner,
I wished i met you later,
Time doesn't work that way, but it works,
If i met you earlier I wouldn't of been ready, if I
met you later i wouldn't know who I know now.
Its funny as much as its seems wrong its
probably the right timing.
Loyal to my heart to a fault my last is still my
last,
Given you everything including the road from
my past,
You have ALWAYS been just right there,
Coincidences that happen too much are fate,
Not the forced kind as we both know all too
well,
It just happens and keeps happening,

We don't know if it's right or wrong but maybe
my soulmates the one who makes me see myself
the most,
I have dreams of how i want my life to go, if i
had to share it with one person I'd always choose
you.
When I told you "I love you" outta everything in
you I know the first thing you thought was
"why"
I felt like I could love you from the first time we
talked,
How our conversation flowed so freely into the
early hours before the sun rise,
We didn't want it to end,
Night in shining armour, you slowly opened
yourself up, possibly unknowingly , I got you a
few times that day,
Called me perfect..got me to blush,
Hours upon hours of just mind stimulating
conversation,
Souls who took to each other we vibed off of
something different,
You are perfection within your imperfections
You are more then who you see yourself as
You are you which is the best thing that could
ever be.
And I NEVER want to see that not be a bigger
part of my life.